Today I am Happy

© Macaw Books

www.macawbooks.com

Printed in India

This morning, Lisa woke up very happy. 'Good morning! I am so happy today!' she whispered to the birds outside her window. 'Cheep! Cheep!' replied the birds. They were happy too.

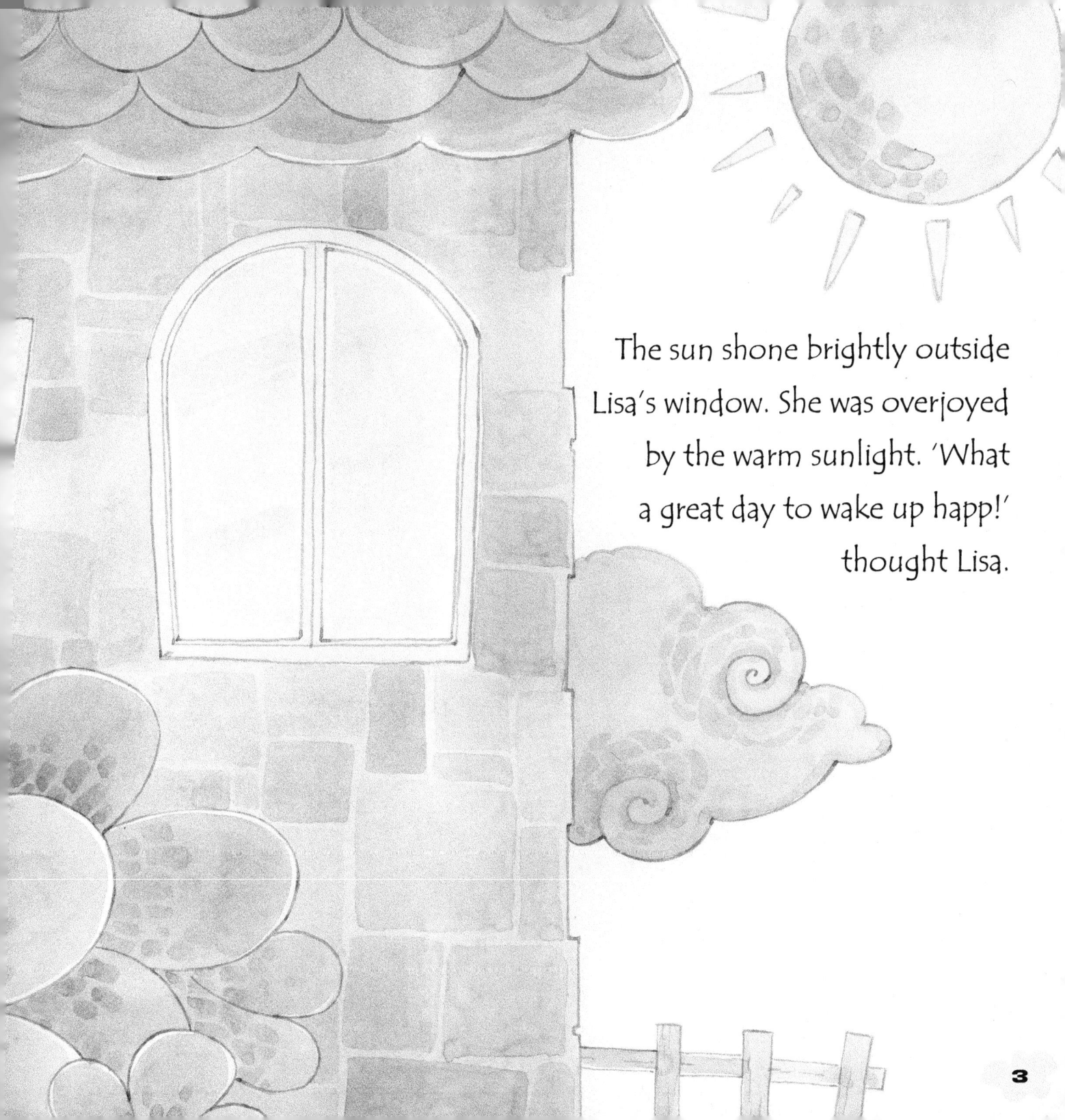

The sun shone brightly outside Lisa's window. She was overjoyed by the warm sunlight. 'What a great day to wake up happ!' thought Lisa.

'I am so happy that my appetite has grown big!' said Lisa. She ate ten ice creams. Their delicious taste made her even happier.

Lisa was so happy that she did a victory jig. 'I am so happy that I feel like a winner!' thought Lisa.

Lisa was so happy that she made up her own song. 'What a happy day is today,' she sang. She skipped out of the house, whistling her new song.

Lisa was so happy that she felt like she could do anything she wanted. 'I feel as great as a king!' she cried. She put on a cape and a crown and walked around the neighbourhood.

Lisa met a few cows grazing in the pasture. 'Hello, cows!' said Lisa. She was happy to see them. 'Moo!' replied the cows. They were happy to see her too.

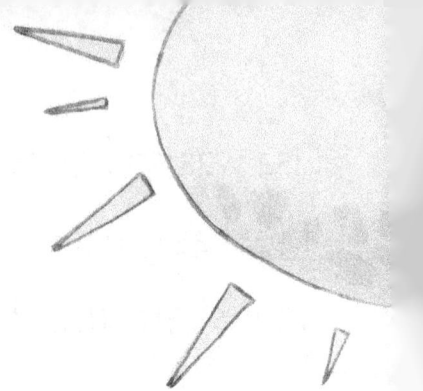

'I am so happy that I could kiss the sky!' shouted Lisa. She jumped up and down with happiness. The sun and the clouds seemed happy too.

Lisa did a few cartwheels out of joy. She had seen the clown at the circus do cartwheels. How happy she was that she could do cartwheels too!

'I am so happy that I feel like I could fly!' cried Lisa. She flapped her arms like the birds that flew above her head. How amused the birds were to see her.

Lisa picked up three apples and began to juggle with them. 'What a wonderful new trick I have learnt!' she thought, proudly.

Lisa was so happy that she caught hold of a branch and swung from it. The little birds in their nest were very surprised to find their tree shaking.

Lisa was so happy that she began to tap-dance in the street.
She clapped her hands and tapped her feet in rhythm.

'Hey! I am a great dancer!' thought Lisa.
She tap-danced the whole way to her
favourite place, the pond.

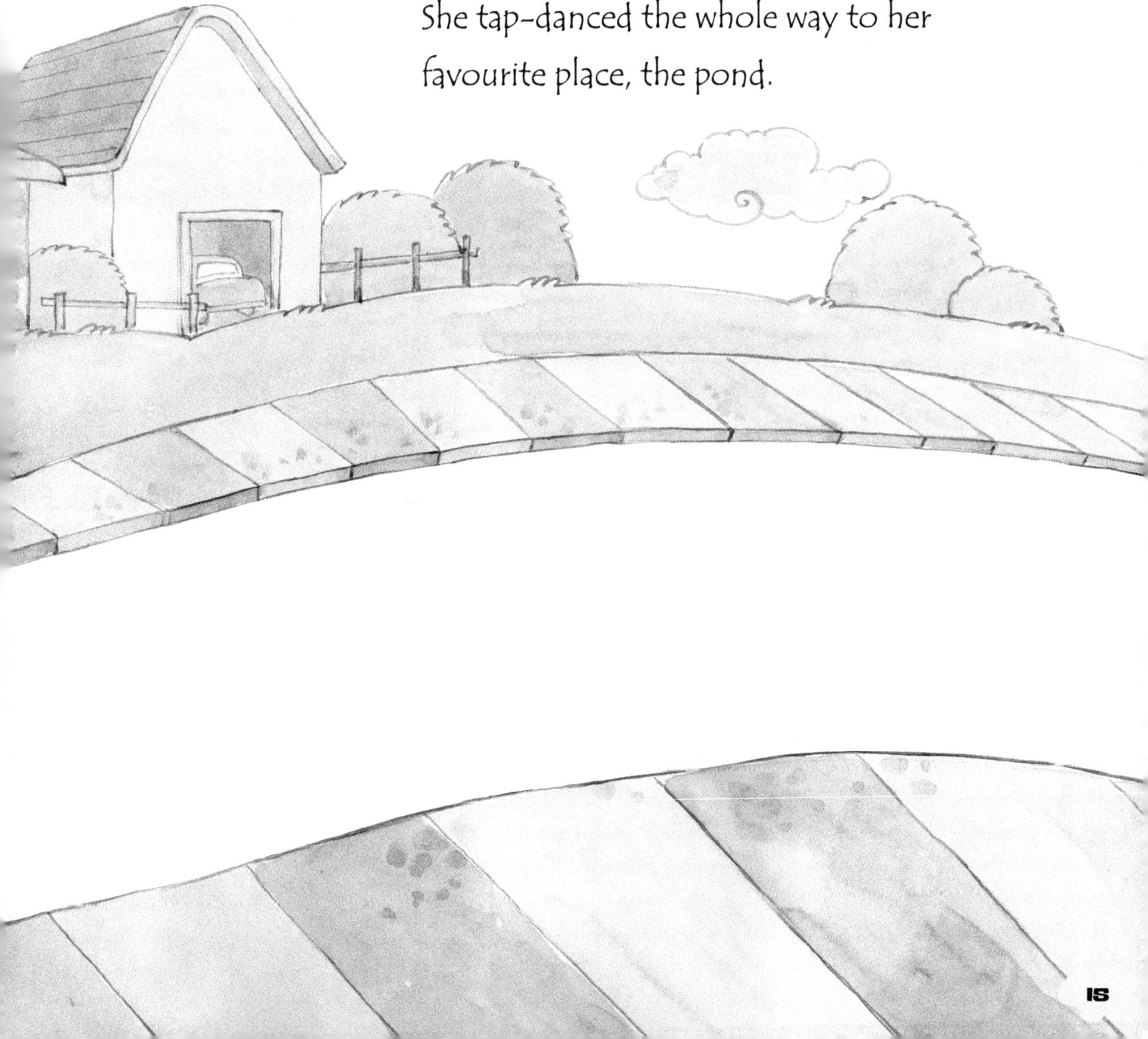

Lisa dipped her feet in the stream happily. The water was cool and soothing. 'What a great day!' she sighed, happily.

When I am
Sad

Heather's brother Bobby was going away to boarding school. Bobby was very excited to be going away, but Heather was very sad. 'I want to go to boarding school too,' said Heather.

'It won't be so bad,' said Bobby, cheerfully. 'Besides, I will be back for the holidays in a few months!' But Heather was still very sad.

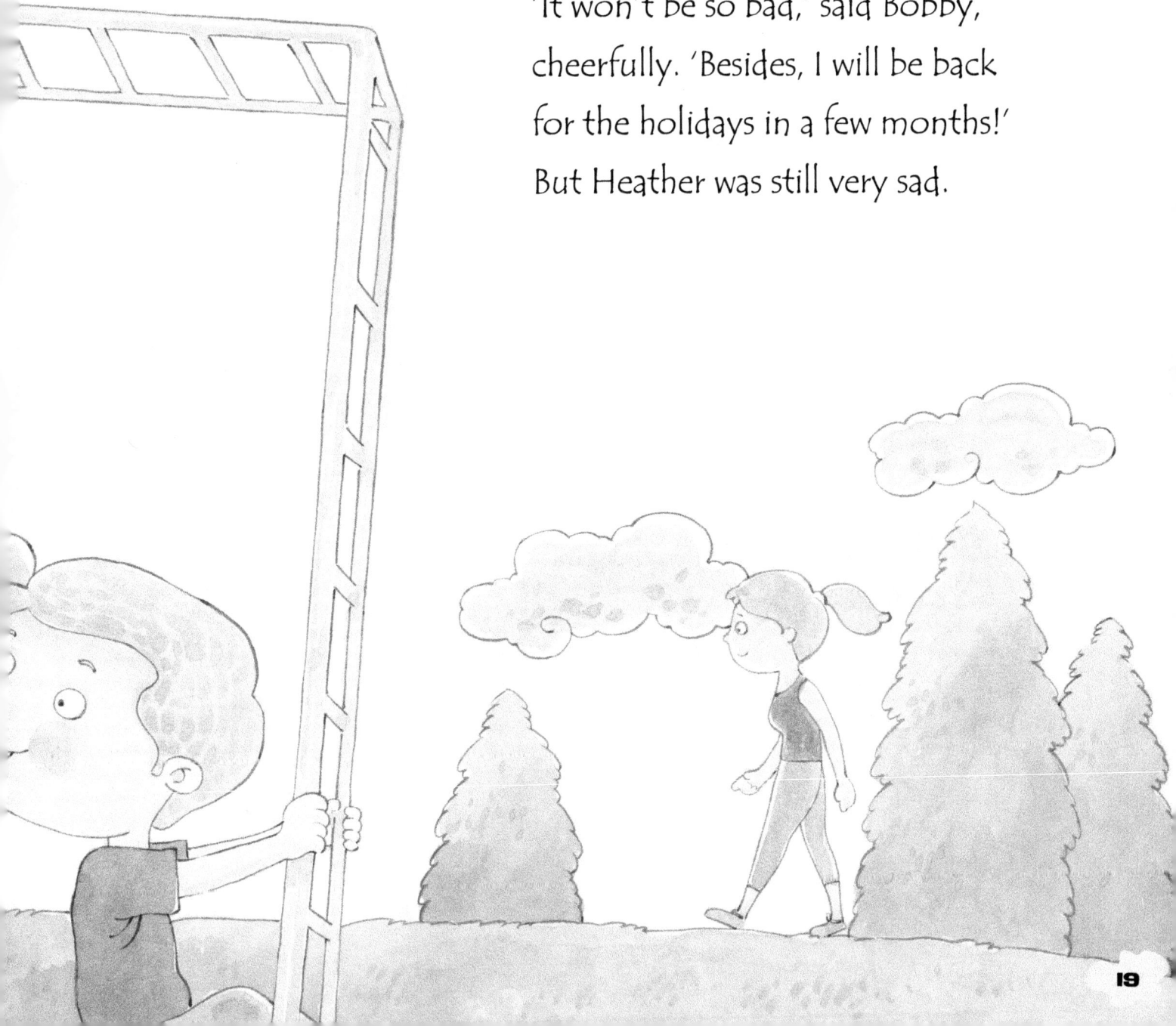

Heather's brother Bobby was also her best friend.
So when he went away, the house felt empty.

The poor girl cried so much! 'I miss Bobby!' she said,
'I feel sad to be at home!'

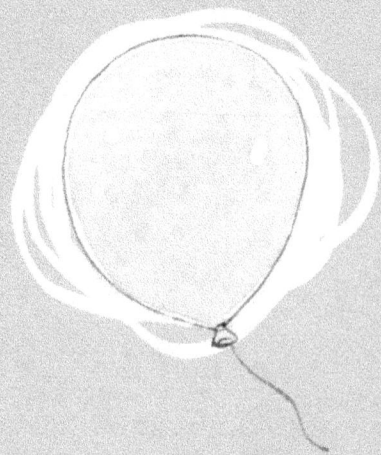

Heather was so sad that her whole world felt grey. She sat in her room and played with her favourite toy. But it did not cheer her up today.

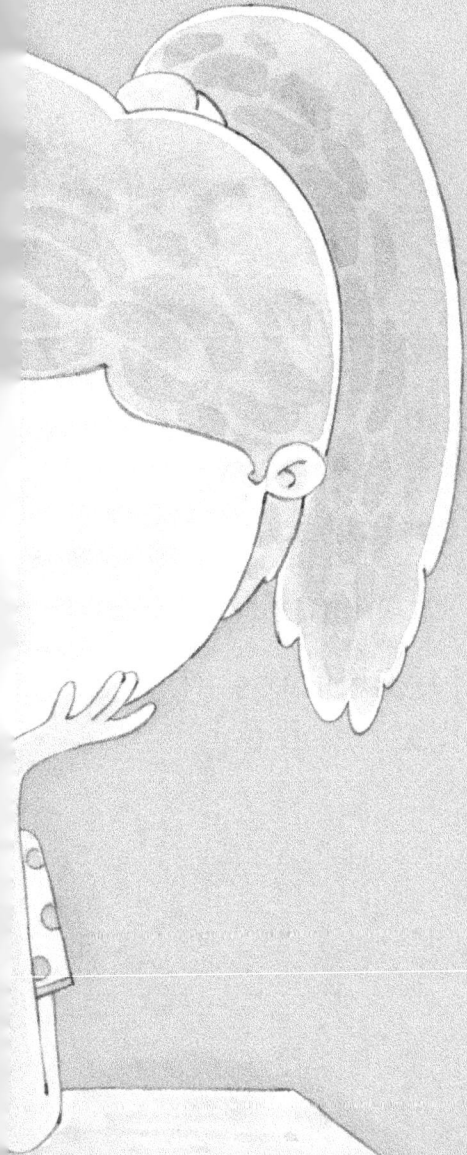

When Grandpa saw that Heather was sad, he got her a balloon. But Heather said, 'Thank you, Grandpa, but I am too sad to play with balloons.'

Daddy put on a clown costume and did funny tricks. He even got a large bar of chocolate for her. But Heather was still sad.

Mummy took Heather out on a nice long ride. As they drove past the shops in town, she felt less sad.

When Heather returned home, she stood in her balcony. The birds chirped happily.

Heather watched the world for a long time and felt a little better. 'It's not so bad to be home after all,' she said to herself.

Then Heather decided to take a walk. She soon reached the meadows where a few lambs were grazing.

A little lamb nuzzled Heather gently. How surprised she was! 'Well, hello there,' she said to the lamb, 'It is nice to meet you too. Let us both be friends.'

When Heather returned home, she was feeling much better. Heather told her parents, 'I don't want to go away after all.' Daddy gave Heather a piggyback ride, and she felt even better.

'I am glad you don't want to leave, darling, because then who would eat this strawberry cake I made?' said Mummy.

The tasty cake cheered
Heather up. When Heather
was quite full, she lay down
in the garden. She felt quite
lucky for Mummy and
Daddy and all the good
things in her life. Heather
was no longer sad.

www.ingramcontent.com/pod-product-compliance
Lightning Source LLC
LaVergne TN
LVHW061249060426
835508LV00018B/1563

2 in 1 Stories

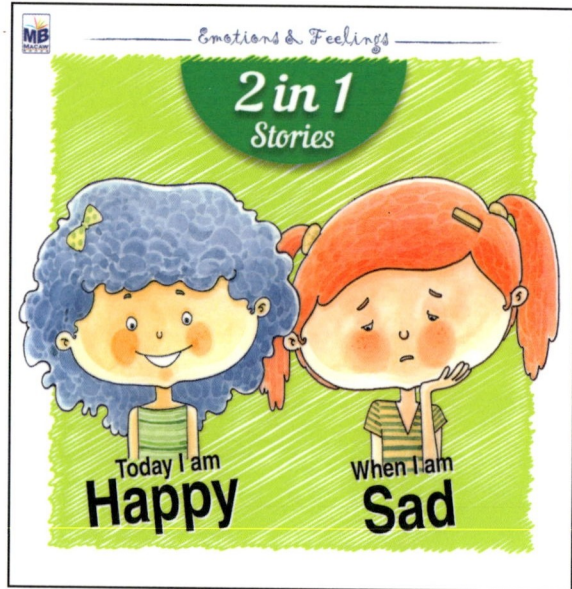

www.macawbooks.com

ISBN 978-1-64035-799-0

9 781640 357990

Yoga Kids
from Acro to Zen

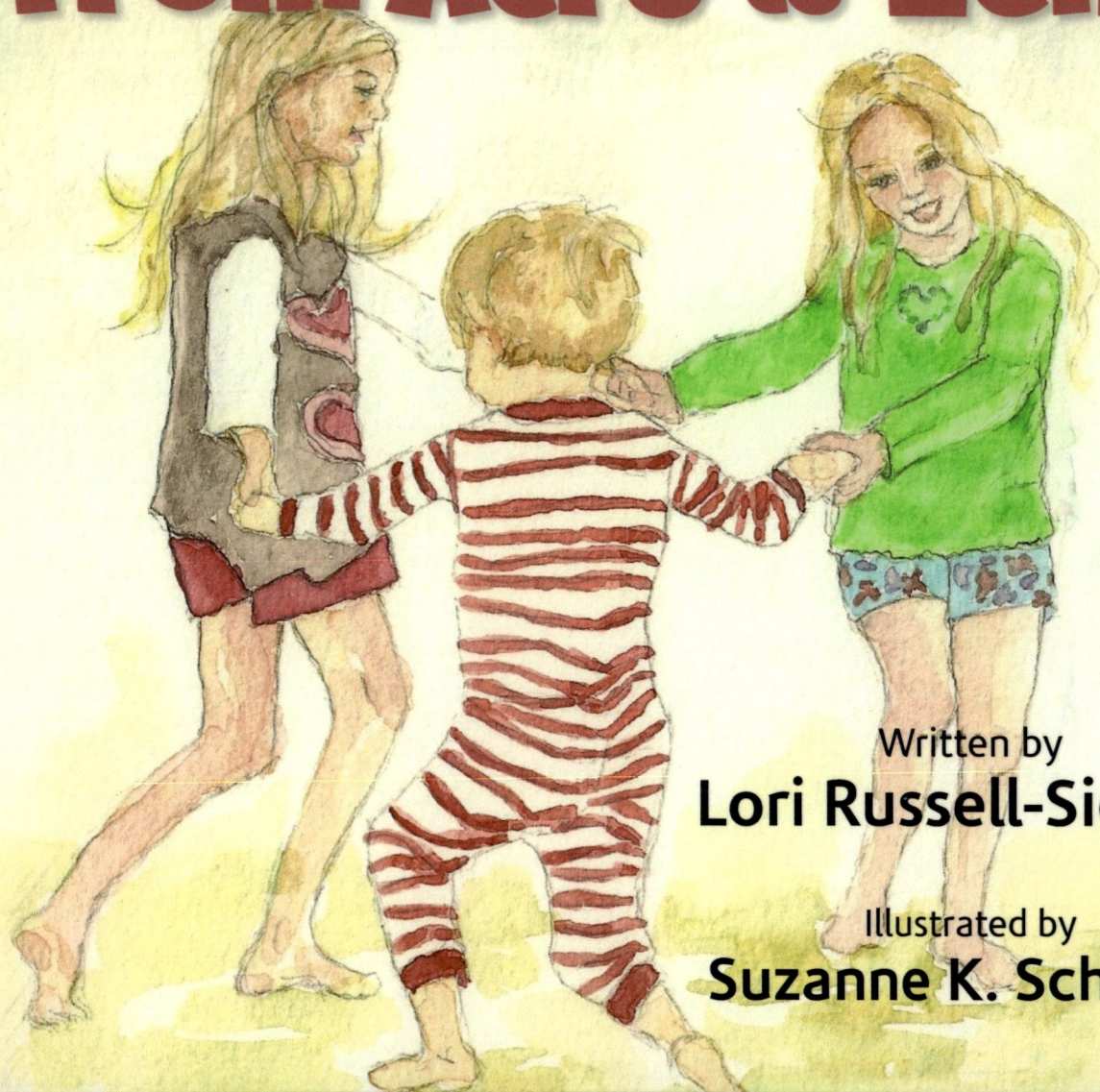

Written by
Lori Russell-Siemer

Illustrated by
Suzanne K. Schmidt